Africa Rising or A Continent

Under Conquest?

Who is benefitting from Africa's growth prosperity narrative?

Many used to consider Africa hopeless, corrupt, dysfunctional, and a difficult place to do business. However, negative perceptions are changing and Africa is now considered a key player in global growth. Foreign investment is pouring in and foreign powers are showing strong interest in re-exploiting the wealthiest continent on the planet.

The global business media is covering more of the region and forecasts have shifted from hopeless to hopeful. The French, Americans, Chinese are all in Africa and expanding their influence. For centuries Africa was treated like a chessboard by competing global powers but for a moment, about half a century ago, it seemed that there was a sliver of hope that somewhere, between the darkness of colonialism and the horrors of an emerging cold war, popular movements were winning independence, taking matters into their hands. Africa was rising! But then the Cold War killed the dream. Moscow and Washington divided the continent into new spheres of influence.

Proxy wars plunged the continent into civil war, but two decades after the Cold War it seemed that Africa is ascending once again and investments are flowing in. The important question is:

Are Africans at last taking matters into their own hands or is this just another Scramble for Africa?

Let's take Kenya for example: Nairobi by old African standards is a young colonial city built on the railway towards the port of Mombasa. Today Nairobi is vibrant. It's a financial and trade hub of East Africa where you will see trucks and cranes everywhere and developers at work, except they're not from the West. They're from the East. China is now Africa's biggest trading partner. In just 10 years, China's trade with the continent has grown from 10 billion to over

200 billion dollars.

At least 2,500 Chinese companies are operating in Africa and more than a million Chinese nationals have moved to do business in Kenya. Chinese companies are visible everywhere but they are remarkably inconspicuous.

In recent years we saw African heads of state celebrate the Chinese-built expansion to the port of Mombasa which would be linked to a Chinese built railway connecting five East African countries. There are ports already in every African country that has an oceanfront and those ports were built by another imperial power, one or another, in the last century. This is simply what imperial powers do. They build ports so that they can send their goods to that country and so that they can export from that country to their markets the things they need from that country.

It is true that Africa desperately needs infrastructure. Whether it needs infrastructure on these terms is the question. African leaders are negotiating many of these deals on the basis of a kind of barter i.e. secure supply of resources for a piece of infrastructure.

Most people elsewhere are not doing that kind of trade or investment with Africa. In addition, China is creating these very powerful feedback loops for its own victory which cuts African countries out of the equation in terms of the benefits. The situation is far from a win-win. For example, blueprints and engineering intelligence is not turned over to Africans. All that important IP remains with the Chinese. The workers they send over pretty much handle most of the work even down to pushing wheelbarrows. Essentially, the loans, plans, materials, designs, the implementations and the workers are to a greater extent all Chinese. Salaries of the workers are typically or at least very often banked in China. So 'win-win' is a propaganda slogan. It's not an accurate description of this sort of arrangement.

Is Africa now run by post structural adjustment oligarchs?

Imperialism evolves. It's different from age to age. The circumstances change. What doesn't change is the balance of power between the two parties that are engaged in imperialism i.e. the weak and the strong. The weaker has an inability to resist or a lack of alternatives. We ought to be skeptical of the whole Africa rising narrative. What civilization can one reference that has ever been developed by foreigners?

What you have is the creation of an elite class that are benefiting from all the investments and also benefiting from the studying of the land. Africa is now run by post structural adjustment oligarchs.

There are several ways of looking at Africa's so-called growth prosperity. In 2018, 8 countries in Africa were in the top 20 list of countries in the world by real GDP growth rate. However, when you look deeper, this is a false go on Africa's growth. It is fuelled by debt and the mass sale of natural resources. Yes, Africa is growing but who is benefiting - Africans and their majorities or only a few oligarchs? Only the elite linked to global finance and global power!

This is now the perfect time for Africa to become what China was many years ago but instead leaders are signing contracts that say 70 percent of the labour for all these projects is going to be Chinese. Some argue that countries globally have moved their productions into China and that across Africa there's no infrastructure project the Chinese take on without it being put on a tender but we know that even before the process starts; because they're providing the credit, they're the ones who are ready to do the barter and they are ready to undercut other bidders' prices because they have a long-term plan.

There are things that countries can do as government and there are things that they need to do with support of private capital or foreign capital so it's fair to make the grounds convenient and conducive for people to want to come and invest in Africa but for the time being this is all theory.

Global powers have long projected their fantasies and fears on Africa. The continent presents expanding markets, cheap labour and natural resources. On the other hand, it's the incubator of their worst nightmares – instability, ethnic conflicts and so-called global terrorism.

With the drawdown in Iraq and Afghanistan, the US war on terror was reported to have pivoted to Africa and around 2013 we saw the US Africa Command run over 400 missions in more than 35 African nations. But the threat of terrorism was initially greatly exaggerated both by the US military and by African leaders.

So now you have these very dictatorial governments

basically branding any civil society movement that has a complaint against the government as sort of terrorists. Today's Africa security agenda is not set in Nairobi or Lagos; it's set in Washington. On the one hand the US wants to fight extremism but on the other hand they want to support military dictatorships or military regimes. What is America's interest in Africa? Well, there's the security agenda and a growing economic agenda.

There's also the competition for political ideas and ideologies i.e. the Scramble with the Americans, Chinese and the French. The French claim to help Africans build democratic institutions, the Americans declare a willingness to help Africans build security structures and the Chinese claim to want to help

Africans build the economic infrastructure.

But the big question is: are Africans benefiting from the new competition or are they being squeezed by this new scramble? The Chinese are living their dream; the Western countries are doing the same while Africans are being forced to live other people's dreams. Africa is living the China dream now. We've been living the Western country dreams but now China is here with its dream.

It's yet to be clear whether Africa will leave its own grave. We need to distinguish what the African agenda is. It's become very fashionable for African governments to talk about a new policy of looking east. The question is whether they are looking east or whether the Chinese are looking to Africa?

Are Africans benefitting from the Chinese engagements in Africa? African governments are now free to actually make deals on terms that are that they can live with which is a step forward from the European and Western relationships since it is creating opportunities for for African governments to begin dreaming about a new infrastructure of modernization. When Western countries were coming to Africa they came in the name of threat.

As Africans we should ask ourselves - when we talk about industries - who is running the industries in Africa? We are a continent that is emerging from an era of intellectual surrender. Intellectual policies are where the entire economic outlook and orientation is externalized. What is encouraging especially for political the elite about China is that we are freed from the conditionality regime that governed this continent for so long.

The continent of Africa is a major focal point for several nations around the world. To a greater extent today than in recent years, perhaps, but certainly to a greater extent than many people realise.

From the US to Russia to Israel to Japan, governments are positioning resources both civilian and military in various African nations, and for various reasons. Who are the players on the continent? What do they want? What does this mean for the future of Africa, for the future of Africans?

To get a little bit of background, the interest in the continent of Africa by foreign powers stretches back several hundred years to the advent of the European slave trade. The extraction of millions of Africans to feed the capitalists project in the so-called new world. When we talk about European slave trade, whether we're talking about the Berlin Conference of 1884-1885, where European powers established the spheres of influence on the African continent and carved up the great big pie, what we've seen is a continued interest. The most accurate way to describe today is that it's just a different phase of the exploitation of the African continent. It's a different phase also of the struggle by Africans for liberation, struggle by Africans to extricate ourselves from the nearly 500 years of European exploitation and European domination. It's a different phase where we need a clear understanding that we are we've been in a 500 year struggle for self-determination on African continent in order to figure out a way forward as a united continent.

Today people see China's increased presence on the continent as similar to the centuries old tradition of exploitation. However, Xi Jing Ping is no Otto von Bismarck. Bismarck presided over 14 or so European nations including United States and other observers in a carving up of the African continent. That's not what's happening today. Today people of different nations are pursuing their interests as nations.

The challenge for the African continent is for it to unify itself in order to compete on a global scale. Whether they're competing with China or they're competing with the United States, Russia, Japan or whoever. What has happened is that we often look at the continent from an outside view so when John Bolton, now former national security adviser to Donald Trump in 2008 unveiled a Trump policy for Africa and says that Africa – a United States of Africa - is a landscape for a great power competition particularly competition against Russia and China - that's the view that we often look at Africa from, however, what is key is first to reorient that prism through which we see the continent.

How is the continent resisting the encroachment of these great powers as a continent unifying to protect its interests? That's our primary and concern and we've seen a plethora of conferences over the last few years from the recent 2019 Japan Africa development conference, to previous China Africa conferences, Turkey Africa conferences and the upcoming 2019 Russia Africa conference.

Now with all of these conferences - exactly what happens is that you have some 50 odd countries going, representing themselves individually as opposed to one unified bloc representing the interests of the African continent. Rwanda for example with 11-12 million people, how's it going to compete with a China which has a population of over a billion? Equatorial Guinea with just over a million people or Swaziland with just over a million - how are these small countries going to compete?

So the onus is on Africans to unite in a continental block as was espoused by figures. Kwame Nkrumah predicted in many of his books this phase that we're in – this neo-colonial phase where you have African leaders who have control of the political or apparatus but do not control their economy.

We see just that in West Africa's relationship with with the French. The French are one of the most dominant forces on African continent where they have some 13 West African nations in what they call the Franc zone - where the currency of these nations is pegged to the French franc and the euro, and the reserves of these nations are kept in a French bank.

We see that the interests of Africans are not being served. The French have monetary control over West African nations and have a tremendous military presence in West Africa. They were crucial in elections in Ivory Coast. We see French troops in Mali and they remain there. We see French troops in Chad. We saw the government change in Libya led by NATO when Nicolas Sarkozy was at the forefront of that, joined by the United States and its Africa Command. This command established around 2008 tries to present a soft and fuzzy picture saying that it's going to help Africans with humanitarian challenges. But we saw the force and true nature of

Africom in the overthrow of Gaddafi, led by the

NATO alliance in the bombing of Libya - destroying

a stable government and creating nothing but chaos

in not only Libya but in the Sahel including Chad,

Mali, Burkina Faso where you see a great deal of

instability now.

Any objective observer would note that from 2008 to

the present, US military presence on the African

continent has increased almost 2,000 percent but

we've all seen a concomitant and exponential

increase in instability, in terrorism and insecurity. So

one would argue that United States' presence

produces insecurity instead of security.

Africom claims to provide stability or to be a

stabilizing force on a continent. However, it seems it really has been an anchor for other countries to take advantage of instability. The African command which was roundly rejected by almost all African nations. Only one country was in agreement establishing a military base on the continent and that was Liberia. If you look at Africom in the context of the Chinese - increasing Chinese influence on an African continent where China is invested tremendously economically to the point where neither Europe nor the United States can compete on the economic plane with China, the equalizer for the United States of course is to protect the strategic interests on African continent. This is done militarily so that's probably the best way to look at why Africom is present. Military support is not top of

Africa's needs. Investments in infrastructure, education, healthcare and sanitation would be top of that list.

We're looking not at a new neo colonialism, so much as we are looking at world powers like China and Russia, Japan and the United States, Turkey and Israel, and even the United Kingdom using Africa as base of operations to compete with and challenge each other for resources, trade, strategic military and diplomatic positioning.

Why Africa

Africa is the richest continent on the planet in terms of its natural resources. Congo for example has about half of the world's cobalt reserves. Cobalt is vital for the US military industry, aerospace industry, for the burgeoning green energy sector etc. Whether we're talking about battery cells for solar energy batteries or electric cars. Congo and Rwanda also have vast reserves of coltan. In South Africa and Zimbabwe, you have enormous platinum reserves and so forth.

Africa is a resource rich continent. As Walter Rodney lays out in his classic work 'How Europe Underdeveloped Africa', it's the plundering of the African continent that leaves Africans impoverished and dependent. However, the picture that's presented to us by world powers is that if you don't do as if we say, we will cut aid.

Hundreds of billions of dollars are going out the back door through plunder. Years ago the main resource was African bodies. African bodies extracted to develop capitalist industries in the West. Today it's the same thing with natural resources, it's diamond, it's cobalt, the timber and uranium and so forth. The framework is very much the same, where Africa is seen as an outpost for the extraction of natural resources to develop the rest of the world. How does trade translate into benefit for Africans who are the owners allegedly of these resources? How are these resources controlled through trade and commerce from the continent to these countries that are coming into Africa to extract?

Well, we're in a neo-colonial environment with

commodores meaning that leaders who are serving the interests of foreign or finance capital. So the small elite at the top who function really as rent seekers, a classic case we see in Djibouti. There they collect rent for military bases. They collect rent from the Chinese, French, Americans etc. You have these elites and new colonial leaders who have been put in place because a tremendous amount of violence was waged against the true African Patriots like Patrice Lumumba, Félix-Roland Moumié, Kwame Nkrumah and Thomas Sankara.

The commodores have chalets and in Switzerland like Paul Biya for example, the leader of Cameroon who is basically a part-time president and spends the bulk of his time in Europe. His government is propped up by France which supplies it with weapons and trains its repressive forces.

France is the leading foreign investor, with over a hundred French subsidiaries located in all key sectors including oil, timber, construction, mobile telephony, transport, banking, and insurance. These elites function to serve Western interests or global interests and not the interests of their own people.

When they get sick they go to hospitals abroad and don't seek treatment in their own countries. For example Buhari of Nigeria and Mugabe of Zimbabwe who recently passed away in a Singaporean hospital. They can't even serve their own interests because they haven't even developed hospitals to take care of themselves or their children when they get sick.

Most of the elites run enterprises centred around collecting rent from the great powers and basically reign over the people and keep the populations in check. Another way this plays out is seen through the increased militarization of the African continent. What happens is the United States in particular provides military equipment to these African leaders ostensibly to fight terrorism but what the African leaders do is they utilize that equipment in order to crush their populations and keep their populations under control.

Some of them who were trained by these foreign militaries wind up fomenting coups like we saw in Mali in 2012 and what we witnessed in 2015 in Burkina Faso. These are African trained figures who actually initiated coups against sitting governments.

We've got a lot of conflating issues from the 500 years of colonial and now neo-colonial involvement on the continent. We have issues of trade, we have issues of militarism and we have issues of crony capitalism and the installation of comprador classes to control masses of working class and poor people on the continent.

Africa is presented as a basket case in need as opposed to a rich continent that's being exploited. However, there is a growing African youthful population comprising of grassroots anti-imperialists that are revolutionary in nature. There is need for new kind of political education, a dire need for fresh learnings on the workings of capitalism and democracy, and a necessity for proper understanding of power dynamics between Africa and the rest of the world presently and throughout history in order for Africans to unite and form a force that can truly compete and be respected by the rest of the world.